Articles 120, 120b, 120c, 43, and 118, UCMJ – DoD Proposed NDAA FY 11 Amendments, as included in S. 3454 by Senate Armed Services Committee, June 4, 2010

the following new section:

"§ 920b. Art. 120b. Rape and sexual assault of a child

"(a) RAPE OF A CHILD.—Any person subject to this chapter who—

"(1) commits a sexual act upon a child who has not attained the age of 12 years;

or

"(2) commits a sexual act upon a child who has attained the age of 12 years by—

"(A) using force against any person;

"(B) threatening or placing that child in fear;

"(C) rendering that child unconscious; or

"(D) administering to that child a drug, intoxicant, or other similar

substance;

is guilty of rape of a child and shall be punished as a court-martial may direct.

"(b) SEXUAL ASSAULT OF A CHILD.—Any person subject to this chapter who commits a

sexual act upon a child who has attained the age of 12 years is guilty of sexual assault of a child

and shall be punished as a court-martial may direct.

"(c) SEXUAL ABUSE OF A CHILD.—Any person subject to this chapter who commits a

lewd act upon a child is guilty of sexual abuse of a child and shall be punished as a court-martial

may direct.

"(d) AGE OF CHILD.—

"(1) UNDER 12 YEARS.—In a prosecution under this section, it need not be proven

that the accused knew the age of the other person engaging in the sexual act or lewd act.

It is not a defense that the accused reasonably believed that the child had attained the age

of 12 years.

"(2) UNDER 16 YEARS.—In a prosecution under this section, it need not be proven that the accused knew that the other person engaging in the sexual act or lewd act had not attained the age of 16 years, but it is a defense in a prosecution under subsection (b) (sexual assault of a child) or subsection (c) (sexual abuse of a child), which the accused must prove by a preponderance of the evidence, that the accused reasonably believed that the child had attained the age of 16 years, if the child had in fact attained at least the age of 12 years.

"(e) PROOF OF THREAT.—In a prosecution under this section, in proving that a person made a threat, it need not be proven that the person actually intended to carry out the threat or had the ability to carry out the threat.

"(f) MARRIAGE.—In a prosecution under subsection (b) (sexual assault of a child) or subsection (c) (sexual abuse of a child), it is a defense, which the accused must prove by a preponderance of the evidence, that the persons engaging in the sexual act or lewd act were at that time married to each other.

"(g) CONSENT.—Lack of consent is not an element and need not be proven in any prosecution under this section. A child cannot consent to any sexual act, lewd act, or use of force.

"(h) DEFINITIONS.—In this section:

"(1) SEXUAL ACT AND SEXUAL CONTACT.—The terms 'sexual act' and 'sexual contact' have the meanings given those terms in section 920(g) of this title (article 120(g)).

"(2) FORCE.—The term 'force' means—

"(A) the use of a weapon;

"(B) the use of such physical strength or violence as is sufficient to overcome, restrain, or injure a child; or

"(C) inflicting physical harm.

In the case of a parent-child or similar relationship, the use or abuse of parental or similar authority is sufficient to constitute the use of force.

"(3) THREATENING OR PLACING THAT CHILD IN FEAR.—The term 'threatening or placing that child in fear' means a communication or action that is of sufficient consequence to cause the child to fear that non-compliance will result in the child or another person being subjected to the action contemplated by the communication or action.

"(4) CHILD.—The term 'child' means any person who has not attained the age of 16 years.

"(5) LEWD ACT.—The term 'lewd act' means—

"(A) any sexual contact with a child;

"(B) intentionally exposing one's genitalia, anus, buttocks, or female areola or nipple to a child by any means, including via any communication technology, with an intent to abuse, humiliate or degrade any person, or to arouse or gratify the sexual desire of any person;

"(C) intentionally communicating indecent language to a child by any means, including via any communication technology, with an intent to abuse, humiliate or degrade any person, or to arouse or gratify the sexual desire of any person; or

"(D) any indecent conduct, intentionally done with or in the presence of a child, including via any communication technology, that amounts to a form of immorality relating to sexual impurity which is grossly vulgar, obscene, and repugnant to common propriety, and tends to excite sexual desire or deprave morals with respect to sexual relations.".

(c) OTHER SEXUAL MISCONDUCT.—Such chapter (the Uniform Code of Military Justice), is further amended by inserting after section 920b (article 120b), as added by subsection (b), the following new section:

"§ 920c. Art. 120c. Other sexual misconduct

"(a) INDECENT VIEWING, VISUAL RECORDING, OR BROADCASTING.—Any person subject to this chapter who, without legal justification or lawful authorization—

"(1) knowingly and wrongfully views the private area of another person, without that other person's consent and under circumstances in which that other person has a reasonable expectation of privacy;

"(2) knowingly photographs, videotapes, films, or records by any means, the private area of another person, without that other person's consent and under circumstances in which that other person has a reasonable expectation of privacy; or

(3) knowingly broadcasts or distributes any such recording that the person knew or reasonably should have known was made under the circumstances proscribed in paragraphs (1) and (2);

is guilty of an offense under this section and shall be punished as a court-martial may direct.

"(b) FORCIBLE PANDERING.—Any person subject to this chapter who compels another person to engage in an act of prostitution with any person is guilty of forcible pandering and shall be punished as a court-martial may direct.

"(c) INDECENT EXPOSURE.—Any person subject to this chapter who intentionally exposes, in an indecent manner, the genitalia, anus, buttocks, or female areola or nipple is guilty of indecent exposure and shall by punished as a court-martial may direct.

"(d) DEFINITIONS.—In this section:

"(1) ACT OF PROSTITUTION.—The term 'act of prostitution' means a sexual act or sexual contact (as defined in section 920(g) of this title (article 120(g))) for the purpose of receiving money or other compensation.

"(2) PRIVATE AREA.—The term 'private area' means the naked or underwear-clad genitalia, anus, buttocks, or female areola or nipple of another person.

"(3) REASONABLE EXPECTATION OF PRIVACY.—The term 'under circumstances in which that other person has a reasonable expectation of privacy' means—

"(A) circumstances in which a reasonable person would believe that he or she could disrobe in privacy, without being concerned that an image of a private area of the person was being captured; or

"(B) circumstances in which a reasonable person would believe that a private area of the person would not be visible to the public.

"(4) BROADCAST.—The term 'broadcast' means to electronically transmit a visual image with the intent that it be viewed by a person or persons.

"(5) DISTRIBUTE.—The term 'distribute' means delivering to the actual or constructive possession of another, including transmission by electronic means.

"(6) INDECENT MANNER.—The term 'indecent manner' means conduct that amounts to a form of immorality relating to sexual impurity which is grossly vulgar, obscene, and repugnant to common propriety, and tends to excite sexual desire or deprave morals with respect to sexual relations.".

(d) CONFORMING AMENDMENTS.—Such chapter (the Uniform Code of Military Justice), is further amended as follows:

(1) STATUTE OF LIMITATIONS.—Subparagraph (B) of section 843(b)(2) (article 43(b)(2)) is amended—

(A) in clause (i), by striking "section 920 of this title (article 120)" and inserting "section 920, 920a, 920b, or 920c of this title (article 120, 120a, 120b, or 120c)"; and

(B) in clause (v)—

(i) by striking "; indecent assault;" and inserting a comma; and

(ii) by striking "or liberties with a child".

(2) MURDER.—Paragraph (4) of section 918(a) (article 118 (a)) is amended by striking "aggravated sexual assault," and all that follows through "with a child," and inserting "sexual assault, sexual assault of a child, aggravated sexual contact, sexual abuse of a child,".

(e) CLERICAL AMENDMENT.—The table of sections at the beginning of subchapter X of such chapter (the Uniform Code of Military Justice) is amended by striking the items relating to sections 920 and 920a (articles 120 and 120a) and inserting the following:

"920. 120. Rape and sexual assault generally.
"920a. 120a. Stalking.
"920b. 120b. Rape and sexual assault of a child.
"920c. 120c. Other sexual misconduct.".

(f) EFFECTIVE DATE.—The amendments made by this section shall take effect on the date of the enactment of this Act and shall apply with respect to offenses committed on or after such date.

Articles 120, 120b, 120c, 43, and 118, UCMJ – DoD Proposed NDAA FY 11 Amendments, as included in S. 3454 by Senate Armed Services Committee, June 4, 2010

Section-by-Section Analysis

<u>Overview:</u> The Uniform Code of Military Justice (UCMJ; chapter 47 of title 10, United States Code) constitutes the military's criminal code and judicial system for the trial of offenses by courts-martial. Pursuant to Article 36, UCMJ, the President is given rule-making authority to prescribe pretrial, trial, and post-trial procedures, including modes of proof, for cases arising under the UCMJ triable by courts-martial and other specified military tribunals. The President exercises this rule-making authority through Executive Orders that prescribe the Manual for Courts-Martial (Manual) and any amendments to the Manual deemed necessary. In 1984, Executive Order 12473 prescribed the Manual's rules and procedures and called upon the Secretary of Defense to cause the Manual to be reviewed annually and to recommend to the President any appropriate amendments.

The Secretary of Defense causes this annual review to be conducted by a Joint Services Committee on Military Justice (JSC) operating under the direction of the General Counsel and pursuant to Department of Defense Directive 5500.17 to ensure that the UCMJ and Manual fulfill their fundamental purpose as a comprehensive body of military criminal law and procedure. The charter for the annual review process is to propose amendments, as necessary, to the Manual by proposed Executive Order or to the UCMJ by proposed legislation.

The JSC and DoD is proposing a legislative amendment to Article 120, UCMJ, "Rape, Sexual Assault, and Other Sexual Misconduct." This proposal addresses the report and recommendation of the Defense Task Force on Sexual Assault in the Military (December 2009), that Article 120, UCMJ, be reviewed because "Practitioners consistently advised Task Force members that the new Article 120 (effective October 1, 2007) is cumbersome and confusing. Prosecutors expressed concern that it may be causing unwarranted acquittals. In addition, significant issues related to the constitutionality of Article 120's statutory affirmative defense of 'consent' and to lesser included offenses have evolved." This report and similar concerns with Article 120, as amended in 2007, have been raised with members of Congress and their staff, who are looking to DoD to address and remedy those concerns. This proposed amendment to Article 120, UCMJ, addresses those calls for prompt DoD action.

<u>Subsection (a):</u> **AMENDED ARTICLE 120:**

Purpose: Article 120 maintains the focus on offender behavior that was a centerpiece of the 2007 statute. This proposal splits Article 120 into three parts: Article 120 is rape and sexual assault of any person, Article 120b is rape and sexual assault of children, and Article 120c is other sexual misconduct. The statutory treatment of consent has been simplified. Definitions are simplified overall and the number of offenses has been reduced.

Specific Provisions:

Rape: The offense of rape is largely unchanged. The primary difference in this revision is that rape by force is now rape by unlawful force. The word unlawful aligns the definition of force with Assault under Article 128. This will facilitate prosecution of forcible rape cases by simplifying treatment of the issue of consent. Also, the word "commits" was substituted for "engages in" a sexual act, to remove any suggestion of reciprocal engagement in the act by the victim.

Sexual Assault: The offense of Aggravated Sexual Assault is currently one of the most confusing aspects of Article 120. The revision "unpacks" the offense and clarifies what conduct is proscribed. The offense is renamed Sexual Assault to address a court member's reluctance to convict for "aggravated" sexual assault merely because the offense does not, for whatever reason, seem sufficiently aggravated to the court member. Also, since there is no sexual act offense of lesser severity, the term "aggravated" was a misnomer. The revision also removes the focus from the degree of incapacity of the victim and refocuses on the accused's actions. Thus, a sexual act with a person who the offender knows or reasonably should know is incapable of consenting due to intoxication or a mental or physical disability is prohibited.

The definition of sexual assault by causing bodily harm was clarified to note that any sexual act or contact without consent constitutes bodily harm, providing an explicit "no means no" statute. A sexual assault of a victim who is in a state of 'frozen fear' when assaulted may be prosecuted under this subsection. Fraudulent representations that the sexual act was for a medical purpose, or that the accused was some other person, are also prohibited. A sexual act with a person who the offender knows or reasonably should know is sleeping or unconscious is prohibited. Also, the word "commits" was substituted for "engages in" a sexual act, to remove any suggestion of reciprocal engagement in the act by the victim.

The change also helps facilitate the prosecution of cases where doctors or other professionals take advantage of their position to abuse a patient.

Sexual Contact offenses: Aggravated Sexual Contact and Abusive Sexual Contact are mostly unchanged except to substitute "commits" for "engages in" in accordance with the analysis above. Wrongful Sexual Contact is deleted because it is no longer necessary. With the clarified "bodily harm" under Sexual Assault (any offensive touching), Abusive Sexual Contact now also contains an offense for any offensive touching that is sexual contact. This is the same offense that is now separately listed under Wrongful Sexual Contact. Due to the complete overlap, Wrongful Sexual Contact was deleted.

Defenses: The only defense denied in all circumstances under this section is marriage. Rape and sexual assault are offender-focused crimes that are criminal even if the offender is married to the victim. This is a change from the current statute, which allowed marriage as a defense when the victim was incapacitated, even if there was no consent to the sexual act. Otherwise, the accused is free to bring any available defense. This is a change from the current statute, under which the restrictions on consent as a defense, and the manner in which the defense is proven, have resulted in a great deal of litigation and confusion, which is unlikely to be resolved by the decision of the United States Court of Appeals for the Armed Forces in *United States v. Neal*, 68 M.J. 289 (2010).

Definitions in Article 120(t) are renumbered and modified as Article 120(g):

Sexual act includes penetration of the vulva by the penis, and penetration of the vulva by any other part of the body or by a foreign object.

Sexual contact is expanded to include touching any part of the body with sexual intent. Touching may be accomplished by any part of the body, including the hands or the mouth.

Bodily harm is clarified to better explain that an offensive touching includes any sexual act or contact performed without consent. The definition of grievous bodily harm is unchanged.

Force: This definition was simplified and the overlaps with "threaten or place another person in fear" were reduced or eliminated to simplify charging decisions. The Military Judges' Benchbook definition of "unlawful force" from Article 128, Assault, was added.

Threatening or placing that other person in fear: This definition was greatly simplified and the overlaps with force were reduced or eliminated to simplify charging decisions. The ability to carry out the threat was removed as a proof requirement for the government.

Consent: The definition of consent was left generally unchanged. The restrictions on the use of evidence of consent were deleted. The circular language in the current law using nearly the same words to explain the interaction of consent and capacity, as were used to define an offense under Sexual Assault, was deleted. The Constitutional and other legal issues that have developed in litigation regarding Article 120, as amended in 2007, are resolved. The treatment of consent is simplified and may be disputed where it is relevant. Categories of persons who may not legally give consent to sexual acts or contact are set forth within the statute to simplify the matters at issue in court. For example, the proposed change makes it clear that sleeping or unconscious persons cannot consent. At least two court members' panels within the last year have acquitted in sexual assault cases due to confusion over this issue. Persons subjected to a fraudulent representation of a professional purpose to accomplish the act, or under the belief that the person committing the act is another person, cannot consent because they do not understand to what they are consenting. Lack of consent was made a permissive inference based on the circumstances of the offense.

Subsection (b): NEW ARTICLE 120b:

Purpose of proposed changes: This section (Article 120b) of the proposed three-section modification of Article 120 covers sexual offenses against children (any person who has not attained the age of 16 years). It simplifies the language in the current Article 120 for rape of children over 12 to make the requirements for proving such a rape appropriate to children rather than the current standard of a reasonable adult victim. The definitions of prohibited sexual acts, sexual contact, and lewd acts are broadened to cover all possible sexual offenses against children currently covered under several confusing and disparate subsections of Article 120. It should be noted that what would be a fourth section to Article 120 offenses, Article 120a, "Stalking," already exists.

Specific provisions:

Articles 120, 120b, 120c, 43, and 118, UCMJ – DoD Proposed NDAA FY 11 Amendments, as included in S. 3454 by Senate Armed Services Committee, June 4, 2010

Rape. Sexual acts defined as rape now include penetration by objects. Any sexual act with a child under 12 is rape, and is a strict liability offense. This is identical to long-standing military law under older carnal knowledge provisions and the current Art. 120, except the definition of rape is broadened to include to include penetration by objects. The defense of mistake of fact as to age is eliminated for cases involving rape of a child. Marriage is eliminated as a defense to rape of a child under any circumstances. It is not acceptable to rape any person, even if that person is your spouse. Additionally, sexual activity is not appropriate with children under 12.

Rape of a child over 12 requires some use of force together with the sexual act. The types of force required are similar to those for adults, but with lower thresholds given that the victim is a child. Unlike offenses against adults, consent is not at issue because children cannot consent as a matter of law. Although reworded for clarity, there is ultimately no substantive change in long-standing military law regarding the offense of rape of a child. The substantive change from the current Article 120 is to correct the use of adult standards of force when the victim is a child.

Sexual Assault. This is the same as the current Article 120. Strict liability for any sexual act with a child over 12 years, except the accused has a defense of mistake of fact as to age, which the accused must prove by a preponderance of evidence.

Sexual Abuse. Sexual Abuse combines several offenses into one. This combination of offenses was intended to capture the gravamen of the offenses while maintaining the simplicity that was desired for counsel, judges and members. Any lewd act with a child of any age is punishable under this subsection. The defense of mistake of fact as to age is available when the child is over 12 years, which the accused must prove by a preponderance of evidence. "Lewd act" is defined to include all sexual contact, indecent exposure to a child, communicating indecent language to a child, and indecent conduct with or in the presence of a child. Exposure, communication, and indecent conduct now include offenses committed via any communication technology to encompass offenses committed via the internet, cell phones, and other modern forms of communication. This fixes the current requirement under indecent liberties that only conduct committed in the physical presence of a child is punishable; this has made prosecution of cases difficult where, for example, an accused masturbates in front of a child via webcam.

Consent. Subsection (f) explicitly states that lack of consent need not be proven for any sexual offense against a child and that a child may not consent as a matter of law. This is the same as current law.

Subsection (c): NEW ARTICLE 120c:

Purpose of proposed changes: The proposed Article 120c captures non-consensual sexual misconduct offenses that subject an offender to sex offender registration. It is the third of three distinct sex crime sections derived from Article 120, as amended in 2007, and captures those offenses that are something other than rape and sexual assault of adults (Art. 120) or rape, sexual assault and sexual abuse of children (Art. 120b). Note that Article 120a is the offense of stalking, a provision unaffected by the proposed amendments to Art. 120.

Specific provisions:

Indecent Viewing, Visual Recording, or Broadcasting. This offense clarifies the offense previously covered by Article 120(k)—Indecent act. It makes clear that both viewing and recording are offenses. It also explicitly creates an offense for distribution of any recording made in violation of the statute, which is not clearly prohibited under the current statute. A generic "indecent acts" provision, identical to what existed under Article 134 prior to the 2007 amendments, would also be proposed by Executive Order amendment to Part IV, "Punitive Articles," of the Manual for Courts-Martialo as Article 134 listed offenses that would capture other types of sexual misconduct that do not qualify for sex offender registration, but nonetheless violate military law.

Forcible pandering. This provision is clarified, but otherwise remains unchanged from the current Art. 120. Non-forcible pandering and non-forcible prostitution are already specified offenses under Article 134 in Part IV, "Punitive Articles," Manual for Courts-Martial.

Indecent exposure. This provision is changed from the current Art. 120 to take away the limitation based on viewing by persons other than members of the household. If the conduct is obscene under the definition of indecent then the conduct is not constitutionally protected and the accused should not be able to avoid criminal consequences by committing the obscenity towards members of his or her own family. A lesser offense of "wrongful exposure" (public nudity that is contrary to good order and discipline or service discrediting) would be proposed as a specified offense under Article 134 of Part IV, "Punitive Articles," Manual for Courts-Martial.

Definitions. The "private area" definition for the offense of Indecent Viewing includes nudity or someone clad only in underwear.

<u>**Subsection (d)**</u>: **CONFORMING AMENDMENTS:**

    1. <u>**Amendment to Article 43:**</u> This is a technical amendment to Article 43 to conform references to the current Article 120 (Rape, Sexual Assault and Sexual Misconduct) with the proposed revision to Article 120 (Rape and Sexual Assault Generally) and enactment of Article 120b (Rape and Sexual Assault of Children) and Article 120c (Sexual Misconduct).

    2. <u>**Amendment to Article 118**</u>: This is a technical amendment to Article 118 to conform references to the current Article 120 (Rape, Sexual Assault and Sexual Misconduct) with the proposed revision to Article 120 (Rape and Sexual Assault Generally) and enactment of Article 120b (Rape and Sexual Assault of Children) and Article 120c (Sexual Misconduct).

Budget Implications: This proposal would not result in any appreciable increased costs to the Department of Defense as it relates to the administration of the military justice system.

Changes to Existing Law: This proposal would make the following changes to chapter 47 of title 10, United States Code:

CHAPTER 47—UNIFORM CODE OF MILITARY JUSTICE

Articles 120, 120b, 120c, 43, and 118, UCMJ – DoD Proposed NDAA FY 11 Amendments, as included in S. 3454 by Senate Armed Services Committee, June 4, 2010

* * * * * * *

§ 843. Art. 43. Statute of limitations

(a) A person charged with absence without leave or missing movement in time of war, with murder, rape, or rape of a child, or with any other offense punishable by death, may be tried and punished at any time without limitation.

(b)(1) Except as otherwise provided in this section (article), a person charged with an offense is not liable to be tried by court-martial if the offense was committed more than five years before the receipt of sworn charges and specifications by an officer exercising summary court-martial jurisdiction over the command.

(2)(A) A person charged with having committed a child abuse offense against a child is liable to be tried by court-martial if the sworn charges and specifications are received during the life of the child or within five years after the date on which the offense was committed, whichever provides a longer period, by an officer exercising summary court-martial jurisdiction with respect to that person.

(B) In subparagraph (A), the term "child abuse offense" means an act that involves abuse of a person who has not attained the age of 16 years and constitutes any of the following offenses:

(i) Any offense in violation of ~~section 920 of this title (article 120)~~ **section 920, 920a, 920b, or 920c of this title (article 120, 120a, 120b, or 120c)**.

(ii) Maiming in violation of section 924 of this title (article 124).

(iii) Sodomy in violation of section 925 of this title (article 125).

(iv) Aggravated assault or assault consummated by a battery in violation of section 928 of this title (article 128).

(v) Kidnapping~~; indecent assault;~~ assault with intent to commit murder, voluntary manslaughter, rape, or sodomy, or indecent acts ~~or liberties with a child~~ in violation of section 934 of this title (article 134).

(C) In subparagraph (A), the term "child abuse offense" includes an act that involves abuse of a person who has not attained the age of 18 years and would constitute an offense under chapter 110 or 117, or under section 1591, of title 18.

(3) A person charged with an offense is not liable to be punished under section 815 of this title (article 15) if the offense was committed more than two years before the imposition of punishment.

* * * * * * *

§918. Art. 118. Murder

Any person subject to this chapter who, without justification or excuse, unlawfully kills a human being, when he—

(1) has a premeditated design to kill;
(2) intends to kill or inflict great bodily harm;

      (3) is engaged in an act that is inherently dangerous to another and evinces a wanton disregard of human life; or

      (4) is engaged in the perpetration or attempted perpetration of burglary, sodomy, rape, rape of a child, ~~aggravated sexual assault, aggravated sexual assault of a child, aggravated sexual contact, aggravated sexual abuse of a child, aggravated sexual contact with a child,~~ **sexual assault, sexual assault of a child, aggravated sexual contact, sexual abuse of a child,** robbery or aggravated arson;

is guilty of murder, and shall suffer such punishment as a court-martial may direct, except that if found guilty under clause (1) or (4), he shall suffer death or imprisonment for life as a court-martial may direct.

* * * * * * *

§ 920. Art. 120. Rape~~,~~ **and** sexual assault~~, and other sexual misconduct~~ **generally**

      (a) RAPE.—Any person subject to this chapter who ~~causes~~ **commits a sexual act upon** another person ~~of any age to engage in a sexual act~~ by—

      (1) using **unlawful** force against that other person;

      (2) **using force** causing **or likely to cause death or** grievous bodily harm to any person;

      (3) threatening or placing that other person in fear that any person will be subjected to death, grievous bodily harm, or kidnapping;

      (4) **first** rendering ~~another~~ **that other** person unconscious; or

      (5) administering to ~~another~~ **that other** person by force or threat of force, or without the knowledge or ~~permission~~ **consent** of that person, a drug, intoxicant, or other similar substance and thereby substantially ~~impairs~~ **impairing** the ability of that other person to appraise or control conduct;

is guilty of rape and shall be punished as a court-martial may direct.

      ~~(b) RAPE OF A CHILD. Any person subject to this chapter who~~

      ~~(1) engages in a sexual act with a child who has not attained the age of 12 years; or~~

      ~~(2) engages in a sexual act under the circumstances described in subsection (a) with a child who has attained the age of 12 years;~~

~~is guilty of rape of a child and shall be punished as a court-martial may direct.~~

      ~~(e)~~**(b)** ~~AGGRAVATED~~ SEXUAL ASSAULT.—Any person subject to this chapter who—

      (1) ~~causes~~ **commits a sexual act upon** another person ~~of any age to engage in a sexual act~~ by—

(A) threatening or placing that other person in fear (other than by threatening or placing that other person in fear that any person will be subjected to death, grievous bodily harm, or kidnapping); ~~or~~

(B) causing bodily harm **to that other person**; ~~or~~

(C) making a fraudulent representation that the sexual act served a professional purpose when it served no professional purpose; or

(D) inducing a belief by any artifice, pretense, or concealment that the person is another person;

~~(2) engages in a sexual act with another person of any age if that other person is substantially incapacitated or substantially incapable of —~~

~~(A) appraising the nature of the sexual act;~~

~~(B) declining participation in the sexual act; or~~

~~(C) communicating unwillingness to engage in the sexual act;~~

(2) commits a sexual act with upon another person when the person knows or reasonably should know that the other person is asleep, unconscious, or otherwise unaware that the sexual act is occurring; or

(3) commits a sexual act with another person when the other person is incapable of consenting to the sexual act due to—

(A) impairment by any drug, intoxicant, or other similar substance, and that condition was known or reasonably should have been known by the person; or

(B) a mental disease or defect, or physical disability, and that condition was known or reasonably should have been known by the person;

is guilty of ~~aggravated~~ sexual assault and shall be punished as a court-martial may direct.

~~(d) AGGRAVATED SEXUAL ASSAULT OF A CHILD. Any person subject to this chapter who engages in a sexual act with a child who has attained the age of 12 years is guilty of aggravated sexual assault of a child and shall be punished as a court-martial may direct.~~

~~(e)~~**(c)** AGGRAVATED SEXUAL CONTACT.—Any person subject to this chapter who ~~engages in~~ **commits** or causes sexual contact ~~with~~ **upon** or by another person, if to do so would violate subsection (a) (rape) had the sexual contact been a sexual act, is guilty of aggravated sexual contact and shall be punished as a court-martial may direct.

~~(f) AGGRAVATED SEXUAL ABUSE OF A CHILD. Any person subject to this chapter who engages in a lewd act with a child is guilty of aggravated sexual abuse of a child and shall be punished as a court-martial may direct.~~

~~(g) AGGRAVATED SEXUAL CONTACT WITH A CHILD. Any person subject to this chapter who engages in or causes sexual contact with or by another person, if to do so would violate subsection (b) (rape of a child) had the sexual contact been a sexual act, is guilty of aggravated sexual contact with a child and shall be punished as a court-martial may direct.~~

~~(h)~~**(d)** ABUSIVE SEXUAL CONTACT. —Any person subject to this chapter who ~~engages in~~ **commits** or causes sexual contact ~~with~~ **upon** or by another person, if to do so would violate subsection ~~(c)~~**(b)** (~~aggravated~~ sexual assault) had the sexual contact been a sexual act, is guilty of abusive sexual contact and shall be punished as a court-martial may direct.

~~(i) ABUSIVE SEXUAL CONTACT WITH A CHILD. Any person subject to this chapter who engages in or causes sexual contact with or by another person, if to do so would violate subsection (d) (aggravated sexual assault of a child) had the sexual contact been a sexual act, is guilty of abusive sexual contact with a child and shall be punished as a court-martial may direct.~~

~~(j) INDECENT LIBERTY WITH A CHILD. Any person subject to this chapter who engages in indecent liberty in the physical presence of a child —~~
   ~~(1) with the intent to arouse, appeal to, or gratify the sexual desire of any person; or~~
   ~~(2) with the intent to abuse, humiliate, or degrade any person;~~
~~is guilty of indecent liberty with a child and shall be punished as a court-martial may direct.~~

~~(k) INDECENT ACT. Any person subject to this chapter who engages in indecent conduct is guilty of an indecent act and shall be punished as a court-martial may direct.~~

~~(l) FORCIBLE PANDERING. Any person subject to this chapter who compels another person to engage in an act of prostitution with another person to be directed to said person is guilty of forcible pandering and shall be punished as a court-martial may direct.~~

~~(m) WRONGFUL SEXUAL CONTACT. Any person subject to this chapter who, without legal justification or lawful authorization, engages in sexual contact with another person without that other person's permission is guilty of wrongful sexual contact and shall be punished as a court-martial may direct.~~

~~(n) INDECENT EXPOSURE. Any person subject to this chapter who intentionally exposes, in an indecent manner, in any place where the conduct involved may reasonably be expected to be viewed by people other than members of the actor's family or household, the gentialia, anus, buttocks, or female areola or nipple is guilty of indecent exposure and shall be punished as a court-martial may direct.~~

~~(o) AGE OF CHILD. —~~
   ~~(1) TWELVE YEARS. In a prosecution under subsection (b) (rape of a child), subsection (g) (aggravated sexual contact with a child), or subsection (j) (indecent liberty with a child), it need not be proven that the accused knew that the other person engaging in the sexual act, contact, or liberty had not attained the age of 12 years. It is not an affirmative defense that the accused reasonably believed that the child had attained the age of 12 years.~~
   ~~(2) SIXTEEN YEARS. In a prosecution under subsection (d) (aggravated sexual assault of a child), subsection (f) (aggravated sexual abuse of a child), subsection (i) (abusive sexual contact with a child), or subsection (j) (indecent liberty with a child), it need not be proven that the accused knew that the other person engaging in the sexual act, contact, or liberty had not attained the age of 16 years. Unlike in paragraph (1),~~

~~however, it is an affirmative defense that the accused reasonably believed that the child had attained the age of 16 years.~~

~~(p)~~**(e)** PROOF OF THREAT.—In a prosecution under this section, in proving that ~~the accused~~ **a person** made a threat, it need not be proven that the ~~accused~~ **person** actually intended to carry out the threat **or had the ability to carry out the threat**.

~~(q) MARRIAGE.—~~
> ~~(1) IN GENERAL.   In a prosecution under paragraph (2) of subsection (c) (aggravated sexual assault), or under subsection (d) (aggravated sexual assault of a child), subsection (f) (aggravated sexual abuse of a child), subsection (i) (abusive sexual contact with a child), subsection (j) (indecent liberty with a child), subsection (m) (wrongful sexual contact), or subsection (n) (indecent exposure), it is an affirmative defense that the accused and the other person when they engaged in the sexual act, sexual contact, or sexual conduct are married to each other.~~
> ~~(2) DEFINITION.   For purposes of this subsection, a marriage is a relationship, recognized by the laws of a competent State or foreign jurisdiction, between the accused and the other person as spouses. A marriage exists until it is dissolved in accordance with the laws of a competent State or foreign jurisdiction.~~
> ~~(3) EXCEPTION.Paragraph (1) shall not apply if the accused's intent at the time of the sexual conduct is to abuse, humiliate, or degrade any person.~~

(f) Defenses.—An accused may raise any applicable defenses available under this chapter or the Rules for Court-Martial. Marriage is not a defense for any conduct in issue in any prosecution under this section.

~~(r) CONSENT AND MISTAKE OF FACT AS TO CONSENT.   Lack of permission is an element of the offense in subsection (m) (wrongful sexual contact). Consent and mistake of fact as to consent are not an issue, or an affirmative defense, in a prosecution under any other subsection, except they are an affirmative defense for the sexual conduct in issue in a prosecution under subsection (a) (rape), subsection (c) (aggravated sexual assault), subsection (e) (aggravated sexual contact), and subsection (h) (abusive sexual contact).~~

~~(s) OTHER AFFIRMATIVE DEFENSES NOT PRECLUDED.   The enumeration in this section of some affirmative defenses shall not be construed as excluding the existence of others.~~

~~(t)~~**(g)** DEFINITIONS.—In this section:
> (1) SEXUAL ACT.—The term "sexual act" means—
>> (A) contact between the penis and the vulva, and for purposes of this subparagraph contact involving the penis occurs upon penetration, however slight; or
>> (B) the penetration, however slight, of the genital opening of another by ~~a hand or finger~~ **any part of the body** or by any object, with an intent to abuse, humiliate, harass, or degrade any person or to arouse or gratify the sexual desire of any person.
> (2) SEXUAL CONTACT.—The term "sexual contact" means—

(A) ~~the intentional~~ touching, **or causing another person to touch,** either directly or through the clothing, ~~of~~ the genitalia, anus, groin, breast, inner thigh, or buttocks of ~~another~~ **any** person, **with an intent to abuse, humiliate or degrade any person;** or

(B) ~~intentionally~~ **any touching, or** causing another person to touch, either directly or through the clothing, ~~the genitalia, anus, groin, breast, inner thigh, or buttocks~~ **any part** of any person, **if done** with an intent to ~~abuse, humiliate, or degrade any person or to~~ arouse or gratify the sexual desire of any person. **Touching may be accomplished by any part of the body.**

(3) BODILY HARM.—The term "bodily harm" means any offensive touching of another, however slight, including any nonconsensual sexual act or nonconsensual sexual contact.

~~(3)~~**(4)** GRIEVOUS BODILY HARM.—The term "grievous bodily harm" means serious bodily injury. It includes fractured or dislocated bones, deep cuts, torn members of the body, serious damage to internal organs, and other severe bodily injuries. It does not include minor injuries such as a black eye or a bloody nose. ~~It is the same level of injury as in section 928 (article 128) of this chapter, and a lesser degree of injury than in section 2246(4) of title 18.~~

~~(4) DANGEROUS WEAPON OR OBJECT.—The term "dangerous weapon or object" means—~~

~~(A) any firearm, loaded or not, and whether operable or not;~~
~~(B) any other weapon, device, instrument, material, or substance, whether animate or inanimate, that in the manner it is used, or is intended to be used, is known to be capable of producing death or grievous bodily harm; or~~
~~(C) any object fashioned or utilized in such a manner as to lead the victim under the circumstances to reasonably believe it to be capable of producing death or grievous bodily harm.~~

(5) FORCE.—The term "force" means ~~action to compel submission of another or to overcome or prevent another's resistance by—~~
(A) the use ~~or display~~ of a ~~dangerous~~ weapon ~~or object~~;
~~(B) the suggestion of possession of a dangerous weapon or object that is used in a manner to cause another to believe it is a dangerous weapon or object; or~~
~~(C) physical violence, strength, power, or restraint applied to another person, sufficient that the other person could not avoid or escape the sexual conduct.~~
(B) the use of such physical strength or violence as is sufficient to overcome, restrain, or injure a person; or
(C) inflicting physical harm sufficient to coerce or compel submission by the victim.

(6) UNLAWFUL FORCE.— The term "unlawful force" means an act of force done without legal justification or excuse.

~~(6)~~**(7)** THREATENING OR PLACING THAT OTHER PERSON IN FEAR.—The term "threatening or placing that other person in fear" ~~under paragraph (3) of subsection (a) (rape), or under subsection (e) (aggravated sexual contact),~~ means a communication or action that is of sufficient consequence to cause a reasonable fear that non-compliance will result in the victim or another person being subjected to ~~death, grievous bodily harm, or kidnapping~~ **the wrongful action contemplated by the communication or action**.

~~(7) THREATENING OR PLACING THAT OTHER PERSON IN FEAR.—~~
~~(A) IN GENERAL.— The term "threatening or placing that other person in fear" under paragraph (1)(A) of subsection (c) (aggravated sexual assault), or under subsection (h) (abusive sexual contact), means a communication or action that is of sufficient consequence to cause a reasonable fear that non-compliance will result in the victim or another being subjected to a lesser degree of harm than death, grievous bodily harm, or kidnapping.~~
~~(B) INCLUSIONS.— Such lesser degree of harm includes—~~
~~(i) physical injury to another person or to another person's property; or~~
~~(ii) a threat—~~
~~(I) to accuse any person of a crime;~~
~~(II) to expose a secret or publicize an asserted fact, whether true or false, tending to subject some person to hatred, contempt or ridicule; or~~
~~(III) through the use or abuse of military position, rank, or authority, to affect or threaten to affect, either positively or negatively, the military career of some person.~~

~~(8) BODILY HARM.— The term "bodily harm" means any offensive touching of another, however slight.~~
~~(9) CHILD.— The term "child" means any person who has not attained the age of 16 years.~~
~~(10) LEWD ACT.— The term "lewd act" means—~~
~~(A) the intentional touching, not through the clothing, of the genitalia of another person, with an intent to abuse, humiliate, or degrade any person, or to arouse or gratify the sexual desire of any person; or~~
~~(B) intentionally causing another person to touch, not through the clothing, the genitalia of any person with an intent to abuse, humiliate or degrade any person, or to arouse or gratify the sexual desire of any person.~~
~~(11) INDECENT LIBERTY.— The term "indecent liberty" means indecent conduct, but physical contact is not required. It includes one who with the requisite intent exposes one's genitalia, anus, buttocks, or female areola or nipple to a child. An indecent liberty may consist of communication of indecent language as long as the communication is made in the physical presence of the child. If words designed to excite sexual desire are spoken to a child, or a child is exposed to or involved in sexual conduct, it is an indecent liberty; the child's consent is not relevant.~~

(12) ~~INDECENT CONDUCT. The term "indecent conduct" means that form of immorality relating to sexual impurity which is grossly vulgar, obscene, and repugnant to common propriety, and tends to excite sexual desire or deprave morals with respect to sexual relations. Indecent conduct includes observing, or making a videotape, photograph, motion picture, print, negative, slide, or other mechanically, electronically, or chemically reproduced visual material, without another person's consent, and contrary to that other person's reasonable expectation of privacy, of—~~
>   ~~(A) that other person's genitalia, anus, or buttocks, or (if that other person is female) that person's areola or nipple; or~~
>   ~~(B) that other person while that other person is engaged in a sexual act, sodomy (under section 925 (article 125)), or sexual contact.~~

(13) ~~ACT OF PROSTITUTION. The term "act of prostitution" means a sexual act, sexual contact, or lewd act for the purpose of receiving money or other compensation.~~

~~(14)~~**(8)** CONSENT.—**(A)** The term "consent" means words or overt acts indicating a freely given agreement to the sexual conduct at issue by a competent person. An expression of lack of consent through words or conduct means there is no consent. Lack of verbal or physical resistance or submission resulting from the accused's use of force, threat of force, or placing another person in fear does not constitute consent. A current or previous dating **or social or sexual** relationship by itself or the manner of dress of the person involved with the accused in the ~~sexual~~ conduct at issue shall not constitute consent**.** ~~A person cannot consent to sexual activity if—~~
~~(A) under 16 years of age; or~~
~~(B) substantially incapable of—~~
>   ~~(i) appraising the nature of the sexual conduct at issue due to—~~
>   ~~(I) mental impairment or unconsciousness resulting from consumption of alcohol, drugs, a similar substance, or otherwise; or~~
>   ~~(II) mental disease or defect which renders the person unable to understand the nature of the sexual conduct at issue;~~
>   ~~(ii) physically declining participation in the sexual conduct at issue; or~~
>   ~~(iii) physically communicating unwillingness to engage in the sexual conduct at issue.~~

(B) A sleeping, unconscious or incompetent person cannot consent. A person cannot consent to force causing or likely to cause death or grievous bodily harm, or to being rendered unconscious. A person cannot consent while under threat or in fear, or based on the circumstances described in subparagraph (C) or (D) of subsection (b)(1).

(C) Lack of consent may be inferred based on the circumstances of the offense. All the surrounding circumstances are to be considered in determining whether a person gave consent, or whether a person did not resist or ceased to resist only because of another person's actions.

(15) ~~MISTAKE OF FACT AS TO CONSENT. The term "mistake of fact as to consent" means the accused held, as a result of ignorance or mistake, an incorrect belief that the other person engaging in the sexual conduct consented. The ignorance or mistake must have existed in the mind of the accused and must have been reasonable under all the circumstances. To be~~

~~reasonable the ignorance or mistake must have been based on information, or lack of it, which would indicate to a reasonable person that the other person consented. Additionally, the ignorance or mistake cannot be based on the negligent failure to discover the true facts. Negligence is the absence of due care. Due care is what a reasonably careful person would do under the same or similar circumstances. The accused's state of intoxication, if any, at the time of the offense is not relevant to mistake of fact. A mistaken belief that the other person consented must be that which a reasonably careful, ordinary, prudent, sober adult would have had under the circumstances at the time of the offense.~~

~~(16) AFFIRMATIVE DEFENSE.— The term "affirmative defense" means any special defense which, although not denying that the accused committed the objective acts constituting the offense charged, denies, wholly, or partially, criminal responsibility for those acts. The accused has the burden of proving the affirmative defense by a preponderance of evidence. After the defense meets this burden, the prosecution shall have the burden of proving beyond a reasonable doubt that the affirmative defense did not exist.~~

* * * * * * *

§ 920b. Art. 120b. Rape and sexual assault of a child

(a) RAPE OF A CHILD.—Any person subject to this chapter who—
    (1) commits a sexual act upon a child who has not attained the age of 12 years; or
    (2) commits a sexual act upon a child who has attained the age of 12 years by—
        (A) using force against any person;
        (B) threatening or placing that child in fear;
        (C) rendering that child unconscious; or
        (D) administering to that child a drug, intoxicant, or other similar substance;
is guilty of rape of a child and shall be punished as a court-martial may direct.

(b) SEXUAL ASSAULT OF A CHILD.—Any person subject to this chapter who commits a sexual act upon a child who has attained the age of 12 years is guilty of sexual assault of a child and shall be punished as a court-martial may direct.

(c) SEXUAL ABUSE OF A CHILD.—Any person subject to this chapter who commits a lewd act upon a child is guilty of sexual abuse of a child and shall be punished as a court-martial may direct.

(d) AGE OF CHILD.—
    (1) UNDER 12 YEARS.—In a prosecution under this section, it need not be proven that the accused knew the age of the other person engaging in the sexual act or lewd act. It is not a defense that the accused reasonably believed that the child had attained the age of 12 years.
    (2) UNDER 16 YEARS.—In a prosecution under this section, it need not be proven that the accused knew that the other person engaging in the sexual act or lewd act had not attained the age of 16 years, but it is a defense in a prosecution under subsection (b) (sexual assault of a child) or subsection (c) (sexual abuse of a child), which the accused must prove by a preponderance of the evidence, that the accused reasonably believed that the child had attained the age of 16 years, if the child had in fact attained at least the age of 12 years.

(e) PROOF OF THREAT.—In a prosecution under this section, in proving that a person made a threat, it need not be proven that the person actually intended to carry out the threat or had the ability to carry out the threat.

(f) MARRIAGE.—In a prosecution under subsection (b) (sexual assault of a child) or subsection (c) (sexual abuse of a child), it is a defense, which the accused must prove by a preponderance of the evidence, that the persons engaging in the sexual act or lewd act were at that time married to each other.

(g) CONSENT.—Lack of consent is not an element and need not be proven in any prosecution under this section. A child cannot consent to any sexual act, lewd act, or use of force.

(h) DEFINITIONS.—In this section:

(1) SEXUAL ACT AND SEXUAL CONTACT.—The terms "sexual act" and "sexual contact" have the meanings given those terms in section 920(g) of this title (article 120(g)).

(2) FORCE.—The term "force" means—

(A) the use of a weapon;

(B) the use of such physical strength or violence as is sufficient to overcome, restrain, or injure a child; or

(C) inflicting physical harm.

In the case of a parent-child or similar relationship, the use or abuse of parental or similar authority is sufficient to constitute the use of force.

(3) THREATENING OR PLACING THAT CHILD IN FEAR.—The term "threatening or placing that child in fear" means a communication or action that is of sufficient consequence to cause the child to fear that non-compliance will result in the child or another person being subjected to the action contemplated by the communication or action.

(4) CHILD.—The term "child" means any person who has not attained the age of 16 years.

(5) LEWD ACT.—The term "lewd act" means—

(A) any sexual contact with a child;

(B) intentionally exposing one's genitalia, anus, buttocks, or female areola or nipple to a child by any means, including via any communication technology, with an intent to abuse, humiliate or degrade any person, or to arouse or gratify the sexual desire of any person;

(C) intentionally communicating indecent language to a child by any means, including via any communication technology, with an intent to abuse, humiliate or degrade any person, or to arouse or gratify the sexual desire of any person; or

(D) any indecent conduct, intentionally done with or in the presence of a child, including via any communication technology, that amounts to a form of immorality relating to sexual impurity which is grossly vulgar, obscene, and repugnant to common propriety, and tends to excite sexual desire or deprave morals with respect to sexual relations.

§ 920c. Art. 120c. Other sexual misconduct

(a) INDECENT VIEWING, VISUAL RECORDING, OR BROADCASTING.—Any person subject to this chapter who, without legal justification or lawful authorization—

      (1) knowingly and wrongfully views the private area of another person, without that other person's consent and under circumstances in which that other person has a reasonable expectation of privacy;

      (2) knowingly photographs, videotapes, films, or records by any means, the private area of another person, without that other person's consent and under circumstances in which that other person has a reasonable expectation of privacy; or

      (3) knowingly broadcasts or distributes any such recording that the person knew or reasonably should have known was made under the circumstances proscribed in paragraphs (1) and (2);

is guilty of an offense under this section and shall be punished as a court-martial may direct.

    (b) FORCIBLE PANDERING.—Any person subject to this chapter who compels another person to engage in an act of prostitution with any person is guilty of forcible pandering and shall be punished as a court-martial may direct.

    (c) INDECENT EXPOSURE.—Any person subject to this chapter who intentionally exposes, in an indecent manner, the genitalia, anus, buttocks, or female areola or nipple is guilty of indecent exposure and shall by punished as a court-martial may direct.

    (d) DEFINITIONS.—In this section:

      (1) ACT OF PROSTITUTION.—The term "act of prostitution" means a sexual act or sexual contact (as defined in section 920(g) of this title (article 120(g))) for the purpose of receiving money or other compensation.

      (2) PRIVATE AREA.—The term "private area" means the naked or underwear-clad genitalia, anus, buttocks, or female areola or nipple of another person.

      (3) REASONABLE EXPECTATION OF PRIVACY.—The term "under circumstances in which that other person has a reasonable expectation of privacy" means—

        (A) circumstances in which a reasonable person would believe that he or she could disrobe in privacy, without being concerned that an image of a private area of the person was being captured; or

        (B) circumstances in which a reasonable person would believe that a private area of the person would not be visible to the public.

      (4) BROADCAST.—The term "broadcast" means to electronically transmit a visual image with the intent that it be viewed by a person or persons.

      (5) DISTRIBUTE.—The term "distribute" means delivering to the actual or constructive possession of another, including transmission by electronic means.

      (6) INDECENT MANNER.—The term "indecent manner" means conduct that amounts to a form of immorality relating to sexual impurity which is grossly vulgar, obscene, and repugnant to common propriety, and tends to excite sexual desire or deprave morals with respect to sexual relations.

SEC. ___. REFORM OF OFFENSES RELATING TO RAPE, SEXUAL ASSAULT, AND OTHER SEXUAL MISCONDUCT UNDER UNIFORM CODE OF MILITARY JUSTICE.

(a) RAPE AND SEXUAL ASSAULT GENERALLY.—Section 920 of title 10, United States Code (article 120 of the Uniform Code of Military Justice), is amended as follows:

(1) REVISED OFFENSE OF RAPE.—Subsection (a) is amended to read as follows:

"(a) RAPE.—Any person subject to this chapter who commits a sexual act upon another person by—

"(1) using unlawful force against that other person;

"(2) using force causing or likely to cause death or grievous bodily harm to any person;

"(3) threatening or placing that other person in fear that any person will be subjected to death, grievous bodily harm, or kidnapping;

"(4) first rendering that other person unconscious; or

"(5) administering to that other person by force or threat of force, or without the knowledge or consent of that person, a drug, intoxicant, or other similar substance and thereby substantially impairing the ability of that other person to appraise or control conduct;

is guilty of rape and shall be punished as a court-martial may direct.".

(2) REPEAL OF PROVISIONS RELATING TO OFFENSES REPLACED BY NEW ARTICLE 120b.—Subsections (b), (d), (f), (g), (i), (j), and (o) are repealed.

(3) REVISED OFFENSE OF SEXUAL ASSAULT.—Subsection (c) is redesignated as subsection (b) and is amended to read as follows:

"(b) SEXUAL ASSAULT.—Any person subject to this chapter who—

"(1) commits a sexual act upon another person by—

"(A) threatening or placing that other person in fear (other than by threatening or placing that other person in fear that any person will be subjected to death, grievous bodily harm, or kidnapping);

"(B) causing bodily harm to that other person;

"(C) making a fraudulent representation that the sexual act served a professional purpose when it served no professional purpose; or

"(D) inducing a belief by any artifice, pretense, or concealment that the person is another person;

"(2) commits a sexual act upon another person when the person knows or reasonably should know that the other person is asleep, unconscious, or otherwise unaware that the sexual act is occurring; or

"(3) commits a sexual act upon another person when the other person is incapable of consenting to the sexual act due to—

"(A) impairment by any drug, intoxicant, or other similar substance, and that condition was known or reasonably should have been known by the person; or

"(B) a mental disease or defect, or physical disability, and that condition was known or reasonably should have been known by the person is guilty of sexual assault and shall be punished as a court-martial may direct.".

(4) AGGRAVATED SEXUAL CONTACT.—Subsection (e) is redesignated as subsection (c) and is amended—

(A) by striking "engages in" and inserting "commits"; and

(B) by striking "with" and inserting "upon".

(5) ABUSIVE SEXUAL CONTACT.—Subsection (h) is redesignated as subsection (d) and is amended—

(A) by striking "engages in" and inserting "commits";

(B) by striking "with" and inserting "upon"; and

(C) by striking "subsection (c) (aggravated sexual assault)" and inserting "subsection (b) (sexual assault)".

(6) REPEAL OF PROVISIONS RELATING TO OFFENSES REPLACED BY NEW ARTICLE 120c.—Subsections (k), (l), (m), and (n) are repealed.

(7) PROOF OF THREAT.—Subsection (p) is redesignated as subsection (e) and is amended—

(A) by striking "the accused made" and inserting "a person made";

(B) by striking "the accused actually" and inserting "the person actually"; and

(C) by inserting before the period the following: "or had the ability to carry out the threat".

(8) DEFENSES.—Subsection (q) is redesignated as subsection (f) and is amended to read as follows:

"(f) DEFENSES.—An accused may raise any applicable defenses available under this chapter or the Rules for Court-Martial. Marriage is not a defense for any conduct in issue in any prosecution under this section.".

(9) PROVISIONS RELATING TO AFFIRMATIVE DEFENSES.—Subsections (r) and (s) are repealed.

(10) DEFINITIONS.—Subsection (t) is redesignated as subsection (g) and is amended—

(A) in paragraph (1)(B), by striking "a hand or finger" and inserting "any part of the body";

(B) by striking paragraph (2) and inserting the following:

"(2) SEXUAL CONTACT.—The term 'sexual contact' means—

"(A) touching, or causing another person to touch, either directly or through the clothing, the genitalia, anus, groin, breast, inner thigh, or buttocks of any person, with an intent to abuse, humiliate or degrade any person; or

"(B) any touching, or causing another person to touch, either directly or through the clothing, any body part of any person, if done with an intent to arouse or gratify the sexual desire of any person.

Touching may be accomplished by any part of the body.";

(C) by striking paragraph (4) and redesignating paragraph (3) as paragraph (4);

(D) by redesignating paragraph (8) as paragraph (3), transferring that paragraph so as to appear after paragraph (2), and amending that paragraph by inserting before the period at the end the following: ", including any nonconsensual sexual act or nonconsensual sexual contact";

(E) in paragraph (4), as redesignated by subparagraph (C), by striking the last sentence;

(F) by striking paragraphs (5) and (7);

(G) by redesignating paragraph (6) as paragraph (7);

(H) by inserting after paragraph (4), as redesignated by subparagraph (C), the following new paragraphs (5) and (6):

"(5) FORCE.—The term 'force' means—

"(A) the use of a weapon;

"(B) the use of such physical strength or violence as is sufficient to overcome, restrain, or injure a person; or

"(C) inflicting physical harm sufficient to coerce or compel submission by the victim.

"(6) UNLAWFUL FORCE.—The term 'unlawful force' means an act of force done without legal justification or excuse.";

(I) in paragraph (7), as redesignated by subparagraph (G)—

(i) by striking "under paragraph (3)" and all that follows through "contact),"; and

(ii) by striking "death, grievous bodily harm, or kidnapping" and inserting "the wrongful action contemplated by the communication or action.";

(J) by striking paragraphs (9) through (13);

(K) by redesignating paragraph (14) as paragraph (8) and in that paragraph—

(i) by inserting "(A)" before "The term";

(ii) by striking "words or overt acts indicating" and "sexual" in the first sentence;

(iii) by striking "accused's" in the third sentence;

(iv) by inserting "or social or sexual" before "relationship" in the fourth sentence;

(v) by striking "sexual" before "conduct" in the fourth sentence;

(vi) by striking "A person cannot consent" and all that follows through the period; and

(vii) by adding at the end the following new subparagraphs:

"(B) A sleeping, unconscious, or incompetent person cannot consent. A person cannot consent to force causing or likely to cause death or grievous bodily harm or to being rendered unconscious. A person cannot consent while under threat or in fear or under the circumstances described in subparagraph (C) or (D) of subsection (b)(1).

"(C) Lack of consent may be inferred based on the circumstances of the offense. All the surrounding circumstances are to be considered in determining whether a person gave consent, or whether a person did not resist or ceased to resist only because of another person's actions."; and

(L) by striking paragraphs (15) and (16).

(11) SECTION HEADING.—The heading of such section (article) is amended to read as follows:

"§ 920. Art. 120. Rape and sexual assault generally".

(b) RAPE AND SEXUAL ASSAULT OF A CHILD.—Chapter 47 of title 10, United States Code (the Uniform Code of Military Justice), is amended by inserting after section 920a (article 120a)